20 Recipes for Programming PhoneGap

Jamie Munro

O'REILLY®

Beijing · Cambridge · Farnham · Köln · Sebastopol · Tokyo

20 Recipes for Programming PhoneGap
by Jamie Munro

Published by O'Reilly Media, Inc., 1005 Gravenstein Highway North, Sebastopol, CA 95472.

O'Reilly books may be purchased for educational, business, or sales promotional use. Online editions are also available for most titles (*http://my.safaribooksonline.com*). For more information, contact our corporate/institutional sales department: (800) 998-9938 or *corporate@oreilly.com*.

Editors:	Andy Oram and Mike Hendrickson	**Cover Designer:**	Karen Montgomery
Production Editor:	Rachel Steely	**Interior Designer:**	David Futato
Proofreader:	Rachel Steely	**Illustrators:**	Robert Romano and Rebecca Demarest

Revision History for the First Edition:

2012-03-15   First release

See *http://oreilly.com/catalog/errata.csp?isbn=9781449319540* for release details.

ISBN: 978-1-449-31954-0

[LSI]

1331653978

This book is dedicated to my children, Lily and Owen. Watching you guys grow up and learn always inspires me to share my knowledge with others! And of course, to my loving wife, Shannon: without your continued dedication to raising our children, I would never find time to write!

Table of Contents

Preface

About the Book

PhoneGap is a library that allows developers to interface directly with a mobile device through the use of its JavaScript libraries. With the multitude of mobile platforms it is very difficult and expensive to create multiple applications in Java, Objective-C, or other native languages. Through the PhoneGap library, most web developers can convert their existing knowledge of HTML, CSS, and JavaScript into mobile phone applications with very little effort. In this book, I will explore many common features of mobile development and how they are accomplished with PhoneGap. This will include GPS location, maps, media, accelerometers, and much more.

Prerequisites

Many of the examples in this book will use basic HTML, CSS, and JavaScript. The PhoneGap API will be accessed exclusively through a variety of JavaScript variables and functions. When PhoneGap does not provide a standard way for implementing a certain look and feel, the jQuery mobile library will be used as well to accomplish a consistent look across multiple devices.

Before beginning with the recipes in this book, be sure to follow the step-by-step tutorials provided by the PhoneGap Getting Started Guide (*http://www.phonegap.com/ start*) for the device you will be working with.

Once your environment is fully configured, you will also need to download the jQuery (*http://jquery.com/*) and jQuery mobile library (*http://jquerymobile.com/*). Inside of the *www* directory (where the *index.html* file currently resides), two new folders should be created: *scripts* and *css*. The JavaScript files from the two downloaded libraries should then be placed within the *scripts* directory. The CSS file and the *images* directory from the jQuery mobile library should be placed within the *css* directory.

These two libraries are not well supported for older versions of BlackBerry (less than version 5.0), so they will be used sparingly to attempt to maximize the exposure of the code.

I will be working with the Android version of the library; however, we will be focusing on HTML, JavaScript, and CSS at all times, so the process will be very device independent—the purpose of PhoneGap!

Conventions Used in This Book

The following typographical conventions are used in this book:

Italic

> Indicates new terms, URLs, email addresses, filenames, and file extensions.

`Constant width`

> Used for program listings, as well as within paragraphs to refer to program elements such as variable or function names, databases, data types, environment variables, statements, and keywords.

`Constant width bold`

> Shows commands or other text that should be typed literally by the user.

`Constant width italic`

> Shows text that should be replaced with user-supplied values or by values determined by context.

 This icon signifies a tip, suggestion, or general note.

 This icon indicates a warning or caution.

Tools

There are many different Integrated Development Environments (IDE) available on the Internet. I have several different favorites; one for each language that I develop in. When it comes to PhoneGap development, there are currently two clear choices: Eclipse for BlackBerry and Android and XCode for iOS development.

However, recently announced the latest version of Adobe's Dreamweaver is including integrated support for PhoneGap, at the time of writing this book it's too early to tell what capabilities this will provide.

Using Code Examples

This book is here to help you get your job done. In general, you may use the code in this book in your programs and documentation. You do not need to contact us for permission unless you're reproducing a significant portion of the code. For example, writing a program that uses several chunks of code from this book does not require permission. Selling or distributing a CD-ROM of examples from O'Reilly books does require permission. Answering a question by citing this book and quoting example code does not require permission. Incorporating a significant amount of example code from this book into your product's documentation does require permission.

We appreciate, but do not require, attribution. An attribution usually includes the title, author, publisher, and ISBN. For example: *"20 Recipes for Programming PhoneGap* by Jamie Munro (O'Reilly). Copyright 2012 Jamie Munro, 978-1-449-31954-0."

If you feel your use of code examples falls outside fair use or the permission given here, feel free to contact us at *permissions@oreilly.com*.

Safari® Books Online

Safari Safari Books Online is an on-demand digital library that lets you easily search more than 7,500 technology and creative reference books and videos to find the answers you need quickly.

With a subscription, you can read any page and watch any video from our library online. Read books on your cell phone and mobile devices. Access new titles before they are available for print, get exclusive access to manuscripts in development, and post feedback for the authors. Copy and paste code samples, organize your favorites, download chapters, bookmark key sections, create notes, print out pages, and benefit from tons of other time-saving features.

O'Reilly Media has uploaded this book to the Safari Books Online service. To have full digital access to this book and others on similar topics from O'Reilly and other publishers, sign up for free at *http://my.safaribooksonline.com*.

How to Contact Us

Please address comments and questions concerning this book to the publisher:

O'Reilly Media, Inc.
1005 Gravenstein Highway North
Sebastopol, CA 95472
800-998-9938 (in the United States or Canada)
707-829-0515 (international or local)
707-829-0104 (fax)

We have a web page for this book, where we list errata, examples, and any additional information. You can access this page at:

> *http://oreilly.com/catalog/9781449319540*

To comment or ask technical questions about this book, send email to:

> *bookquestions@oreilly.com*

For more information about our books, courses, conferences, and news, see our website at: *http://www.oreilly.com*.

Find us on Facebook: *http://facebook.com/oreilly*

Follow us on Twitter: *http://twitter.com/oreillymedia*

Watch us on YouTube: *http://www.youtube.com/oreillymedia*

Acknowledgments

I'd like to thank my colleague, Peter Hodgkinson (*http://www.peterhodgkinson.com*), for reviewing this book and ensuring that the example code was logically correct and consistent throughout the recipes.

The Recipes

Determining Whether the Device Is Ready

Problem

You want to execute a PhoneGap API call, but you are unsure whether the device is ready and the application will not function if the API attempts to access the device prematurely.

Solution

The core functionalities that PhoneGap makes accessible through the JavaScript API depend on the device being ready; however, JavaScript can begin working as soon as the Document Object Model (DOM) is available. Therefore, before you perform any API call, you must ensure that PhoneGap has determined that the device is ready for use.

There are two solutions for checking whether the device is ready. For iOS, Android, and BlackBerry (version 5.0 and higher), a custom event type that you can attach to the DOM is available, and PhoneGap will trigger this event when the device is ready.

 For older versions of BlackBerry, PhoneGap is unable to fire the custom event, so you must perform a basic JavaScript interval check for a Boolean variable to indicate whether PhoneGap is ready or not.

Discussion

Throughout the recipes in this book, I will always attempt to separate the code as much as possible, meaning that JavaScript will be placed in *.js* files, CSS in *.css* files, and HTML in *.html* files. During the prerequisites mentioned in the Preface, you should have created two folders inside of your *www* directory: *scripts* and *css*.

The core of the JavaScript code will be placed inside of a file called *common.js*. Create this file now inside of your **scripts** directory. Once created, place the following code in the file:

```
// Global variable that will tell us whether PhoneGap is ready
var isPhoneGapReady = false;

function init() {
    // Add an event listener for deviceready
    document.addEventListener("deviceready",
        onDeviceReady, false);

    // Older versions of Blackberry < 5.0 don't support
    // PhoneGap's custom events, so instead we need to perform
    // an interval check every 500 milliseconds to see whether
    // PhoneGap is ready.  Once done, the interval will be
    // cleared and normal processing can begin.
    var intervalID = window.setInterval(function() {
            if (PhoneGap.available) {
                onDeviceReady();
            }
        }, 500);
}

function onDeviceReady() {
    window.clearInterval(intervalID);

    // set to true
    isPhoneGapReady = true;

    alert('The device is now ready');
}

// Set an onload handler to call the init function
window.onload = init;
```

This JavaScript code does only one important thing: it creates and sets a global variable called isPhoneGapReady that will be used in many future recipes before making Phone-Gap-specific API calls.

To know whether the device is ready, PhoneGap creates and triggers a custom window event called deviceready. By listening for this event, the variable can be changed accordingly. The alert is useful for testing, but of course you should remove it for production use.

In the code, I've placed a large block comment underneath the event listener because older versions of BlackBerry do not support creating custom events. Instead, the code must check the PhoneGap.available variable every 500 milliseconds to see if it is ready. Once it is, the interval is cleared and the onDeviceReady function is called the same as what the event listener created previously.

Finally, the *index.html* file must be updated to include this JavaScript file:

```
<!DOCTYPE HTML>
<html>
<head>
<title>PhoneGap</title>
    <script type="text/javascript" charset="utf-8"
```

```
            src="scripts/phonegap-1.0.0.js"></script>
        <script type="text/javascript" charset="utf-8"
            src="scripts/common.js"></script>
</head>
<body>
    <h1>Hello World!</h1>
</body>
</html>
```

 In the HTML sample, the PhoneGap JavaScript file is being referenced inside of the **scripts** directory. Be sure to copy your PhoneGap Java-Script file inside of this directory. Also, you might be required to update the version depending on the latest available version.

You might notice that I've specified an HTML5 **doctype**. Many of the newest phones support a lot of the features of HTML5, which open up a whole world of possibilities to create cross-platform interactivity.

See Also

JavaScript Events (*http://www.w3schools.com/jsref/dom_obj_event.asp*)

Retrieving Information About the Device

Problem

You want to add functionality that is available only on a certain device or platform.

Solution

Certain features of the PhoneGap API are only available to certain handsets. To avoid limiting the features overall, by detecting the device type, you can offer different features for iOS, Android, or different BlackBerry versions.

The PhoneGap API exposes a global structure called **device** that contains information about the device, version, UUID, platform, and name. Each property can be accessed through JavaScript.

Discussion

There are quite obviously a lot of differences among the various smartphones today. Because of these differences, it's important to be aware of what device your application is running on. At all times, our goal is to have to maintain only one codeset, but that doesn't mean that you cannot add additional features that specific phones support.

Below are some basic JavaScript examples of how you can access each property available in the device structure:

```
var deviceName = device.name;
var deviceVersion = device.version;
var devicePlatform = device.platform;
var deviceUUID = device.uuid;
var phoneGapVersion = device.phonegap;
```

Nothing too special is happening here; each property is being stored to a global variable.

The following example retrieves the device's platform information after PhoneGap informs the application that the device is ready. Based on the information returned, the code sets a global variable that can be used in future code examples to target device-specific implementations:

```
// Global variable that will tell us whether PhoneGap is ready
var isPhoneGapReady = false;

// Default all phone types to false
var isAndroid = false;
var isBlackberry = false;
var isIphone = false;
var isWindows = false;

// Store the device's uuid
var deviceUUID;

function init() {
    // Add an event listener for deviceready
    document.addEventListener("deviceready",
        onDeviceReady, false);
}

function onDeviceReady() {
    // set to true
    isPhoneGapReady = true;

    deviceUUID = device.uuid;

    // detect the device's platform
    deviceDetection();
}

function deviceDetection() {
    if (isPhoneGapReady) {
        switch (device.platform) {
            case "Android":
                isAndroid = true;
                break;
            case "Blackberry":
                isBlackberry = true;
                break;
            case "iPhone":
                isIphone = true;
```

```
            break;
        case "WinCE":
            isWindows = true;
            break;
    }

    alert("Detected you are using a " + device.platform);
    }
}

// Set an onload handler to call the init function
window.onload = init;
```

Most of the code is the same as the first recipe, with a few notable additions. Firstly, several global Boolean variables are defined, one for each of the possible phone types. They all default to `false`, as no detection has been performed yet.

 In the above code sample, the interval device-ready check for older versions of BlackBerry has been removed. If you wish to release your application targeting this version, it should be left in.

Next, inside of the `onDeviceReady` function, the global variable that stores the UUID is set. Right beneath this is a function call to `deviceDetection`. Inside of this function, a switch statement is performed on the `device.platform`. Based on the case statement that is matched, the accompanying Boolean variable is set to true for that platform.

In future recipes, if you wish to target iPhone or Android platforms only, you can perform a simple `if` statement as follows:

```
if (isAndroid) {
    // Do something for Android only...
}
```

Creating a Persistent Navigation System

Problem

You want to allow the user to navigate to other pages while providing a persistent menu at the bottom of the application.

Solution

The iOS has made it commonplace to include a persistent navigation bar that allows one-touch access to frequently used views. Typically, this is located at the bottom of the application.

The beauty of PhoneGap is that it allows you to create mobile applications through the use of HTML, JavaScript, and CSS. The creators of jQuery have created an excellent library called jQuery mobile that helps the user to mimic the native look and feel of menus and buttons on the device using HTML and CSS. By utilizing this library, you can easily achieve the standard footer menu matching the common functionality that smartphone users have become accustomed to.

Discussion

A navigation system is created through some basic HTML links. If you place these links inside a div tag that has some additional data-role attributes applied to it, the jQuery mobile library will convert this to a consistent-looking footer menu. In this example, two links are created, one for home and one for "about." When you run this example on your phone, the code will appear in the footer of your device. Because some Java-Script work is performed to align the menu to the bottom, you might notice that the menu will start to appear higher up, then *jump* down.

```
<!DOCTYPE HTML>
<html>
<head>
    <title>PhoneGap</title>
    <link rel="stylesheet"  href="
        css/jquery.mobile-1.0rc1.min.css" />
    <script type="text/javascript" charset="utf-8"
        src="scripts/phonegap-1.0.0.js"></script>
    <script type="text/javascript" charset="utf-8"
        src="scripts/common.js"></script>
    <script type="text/javascript" charset="utf-8"
        src="scripts/jquery-1.6.4.min.js"></script>
    <script type="text/javascript" charset="utf-8"
        src="scripts/jquery.mobile-1.0rc1.min.js"></script>
</head>
<body>
    <h1>Hello World!</h1>

    <div data-role="footer" data-position="fixed">
        <div data-role="navbar">
            <ul>
                <li><a href="index.html"
class="ui-btn-active">Home</a></li>
                <li><a href="about.html">About</a></li>
            </ul>
        </div>
    </div>
</body>
</html>
```

New versions of the JavaScript libraries are frequently released, so be sure to rename the filename versions in the previous code sample.

Figure 1 is an example of what the jQuery mobile library produces on my Android simulator.

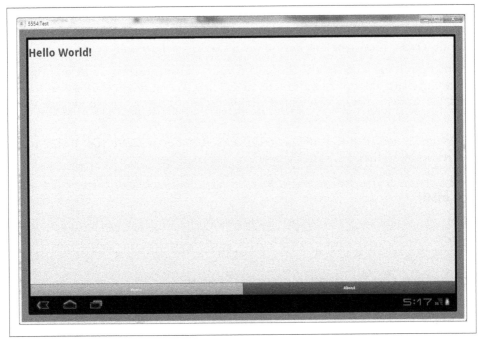

Figure 1. Example footer menu

The key HTML to create this menu are the `data-role` and `data-position` attributes on the two `div` tags surrounding the links. By changing these values, you can alter the menu to appear on top, or make it float by removing the fixed position.

If you wish to style your menu a bit more, several other features can be added. For instance, you can add an icon above each link by applying the `data-icon` attribute to the link tag. The jQuery library contains a variety of predefined icons (*http://jquerymo bile.com/demos/1.0rc1/docs/buttons/buttons-icons.html*). If you wish to use your own icons, this can be accomplished as follows:

```
<style>
    .ui-icon-home-custom {
        background-image: url(images/home-icon.png);
    }
</style>

<div data-role="footer" data-position="fixed">
    <div data-role="navbar">
        <ul>
            <li><a href="index.html" data-icon="home-custom"
                class="ui-btn-active">Home</a></li>
            <li><a href="about.html">About</a></li>
```

```
        </ul>
      </div>
    </div>
```

The home-icon.png should be saved as a PNG-8 and be 18×18 pixels in dimension, with alpha transparency. You don't have to conform to this convention, but it will help provide a more consistent look in case you use some of the built-in icons.

Another great way to customize the look of your navbar is to alter the default theme. By adding a data-theme attribute to your menu links, you can adjust the color and styles used. Currently, jQuery comes with five built-in themes. Simply set the attribute value a, b, c, d, or e to adjust the theme.

Of course, if you wish to really get creative, you can even create your own custom theme; however, that is outside the scope of this book.

See Also

Theming Toolbars (*http://jquerymobile.com/demos/1.0/docs/toolbars/bars-themes.html*)

Detecting the Device's Network Status

Problem

You want to retrieve or send data using the device's network connection from the application; however, the application doesn't know whether the user has network access.

Solution

Before you attempt to access content from the Internet, it's important to ensure that the user has Internet access. The app stores won't accept applications that don't display standard error messages or warnings when the user is not connected to the Internet and content cannot be retrieved.

The PhoneGap API exposes a connection type variable that detects the device's current network status. Several constants are available that provide further detail regarding the device's network status, allowing for potential content scaling for users on a slower network or with low bandwidth plans.

Discussion

By ensuring that the variable navigator.network.connection.type is not equal to the constant Connection.NONE, the application is able to determine that the device is actively connected to the Internet. The following example extends the previously created *common.js* file to add a new function that performs this check and sets a global variable to true. This function is called from the onDeviceReady function.

```
// Global variable that will tell us whether PhoneGap is ready
var isPhoneGapReady = false;

// Store the current network status
var isConnected = false;

function init() {
    // Add an event listener for deviceready
    document.addEventListener("deviceready",
        onDeviceReady, false);
}

function onDeviceReady() {
    // set to true
    isPhoneGapReady = true;

    // detect for network access
    networkDetection();
}

function networkDetection() {
    if (isPhoneGapReady) {
        // as long as the connection type is not none,
        // the device should have Internet access
        if (navigator.network.connection.type != Connection.NONE) {
            isConnected = true;
        }
    }
}

// Set an onload handler to call the init function
window.onload = init;
```

This code allows future functions to perform a check to ensure that the device is connected to the Internet prior to making any external calls. The next example will update the networkDetection function to set a new global variable, indicating whether the application is connected to a high-speed connection.

```
// Global variable that will tell us whether PhoneGap is ready
var isPhoneGapReady = false;

// Store the current network status
var isConnected = false;
var isHighSpeed = false;

function init() {
    // Add an event listener for deviceready
    document.addEventListener("deviceready",
        onDeviceReady, false);
}

function onDeviceReady() {
```

```
        // set to true
        isPhoneGapReady = true;

        // detect for network access
        networkDetection();
}

function networkDetection() {
    if (isPhoneGapReady) {
        // as long as the connection type is not none,
        // the device should have Internet access
        if (navigator.network.connection.type != Connection.NONE) {
            isConnected = true;
        }

        // determine whether this connection is high-speed
        switch (navigator.network.connection.type) {
            case Connection.UNKNOWN:
            case Connection.CELL_2G:
                isHighSpeed = false;
                break;
            default:
                isHighSpeed = true;
                break;
        }
    }
}

// Set an onload handler to call the init function
window.onload = init;
```

Now, when you wish to load content from an external server, by determining whether the user has a low-speed connection, you can serve lower bandwidth content to ensure a faster load time. In the previous example, a 2G or unknown connection type determines low speed. This example can be altered to recognize other connection types such as 3G, WiFi, etc., as types of low-speed connection.

See Also

Comparison of Mobile Phone Wireless Connections (*http://en.wikipedia.org/wiki/Comparison_of_mobile_phone_standards#Comparison_of_wireless_Internet_standards*)

Detecting When the Network Status Changes

Problem

In "Detecting the Device's Network Status" on page 8, you detected that the user had network access when the application first loaded; however, in the time since this was initially detected, the application is unsure whether the user still has connectivity prior to making the first network request.

Solution

As a user travels with his or her device, the network status might change, becoming either active or inactive. If your application is network sensitive, it's important to track these changes. You may need to alert the user or implement a sync system to maintain a record of the changes the user makes until the network becomes available again.

The PhoneGap API exposes a variety of events for which an application can listen through a standard DOM event listener. Two of these events are *online* and *offline*, which are triggered when the device's network status changes.

 As discussed in the first recipe, custom events are not supported by BlackBerry devices older than version 5.0. If you wish to support the events we manipulate in this recipe, the best solution would be to implement a similar interval timer that checks the device's network status for changes manually. Unfortunately, that's both programmatically complex and a drain on the device.

Discussion

In the following example, the onDeviceReady function will be updated to add two event listeners: online and offline. When the event fires, a function will be called that will alter the previously created global variable isConnected. This will be done inside the existing *common.js* file:

```
// Global variable that will tell us whether PhoneGap is ready
var isPhoneGapReady = false;

// Store the current network status
var isConnected = false;
var isHighSpeed = false;
var internetInterval;

function init() {
    // Add an event listener for deviceready
    document.addEventListener("deviceready",
        onDeviceReady, false);
}

function onDeviceReady() {
    // set to true
    isPhoneGapReady = true;

    // detect for network access
    networkDetection();
```

```
    // attach events for online and offline detection
    document.addEventListener("online", onOnline, false);
    document.addEventListener("offline", onOffline, false);
}

function networkDetection() {
    if (isPhoneGapReady) {
        // as long as the connection type is not none,
        // the device should have Internet access
        if (navigator.network.connection.type != Connection.NONE) {
            isConnected = true;
        }

        // determine if this connection is high speed or not
        switch (navigator.network.connection.type) {
            case Connection.UNKNOWN:
            case Connection.CELL_2G:
                isHighSpeed = false;
                break;
            default:
                isHighSpeed = true;
                break;
        }
    }
}

function onOnline() {
    isConnected = true;
}

function onOffline() {
    isConnected = false;
}

// Set an onload handler to call the init function
window.onload = init;
```

As I mentioned earlier, this example won't work for older versions of BlackBerry because of the inability to support custom events. If you wish to support these older
versions, the following example contains additional code that will set an interval to
check whether the network connection has changed every 5 seconds. You can alter the
number of milliseconds in your code if you wish to increase or decrease the frequency.

```
function onDeviceReady() {
    window.clearInterval(intervalID);

    // set to true
    isPhoneGapReady = true;

    // detect for network access
    networkDetection();

    // attach events for online and offline detection
    document.addEventListener("online", onOnline, false);
    document.addEventListener("offline", onOffline, false);
```

```
        // set a timer to check the network status
        internetInterval = window.setInterval(function() {
            if (navigator.network.connection.type != Connection.NONE) {
                onOnline();
            } else {
                onOffline();
            }
        }, 5000);
    }
```

Here, inside of the if statement that checks the network connection, I am calling the previously created onOnline and onOffline functions, instead of just changing the isConnected variable. By doing this, I allow future changes to those functions to add additional functionality without changing code in multiple spots.

 Instead of performing an interval check, you can create a function that checks the connection type immediately before executing a request that requires a network connection.

Executing a Callback Function Once the Device Is Ready

Problem

After a page has loaded, you will want to execute some JavaScript code immediately without invoking it manually each time in your JavaScript code.

Solution

Because HTML doesn't allow for a lot of dynamic features, a lot of code needs to be duplicated. To minimize the page load times, you should load the minimal amount of content each time while reusing as much code as you can. The *common.js* JavaScript file must be kept lightweight, and additional JavaScript files should be created for other new functionality. However, there currently is no process to allow for additional function calls once the application has determined that the device is ready.

You can update the *common.js* JavaScript file with an automatic callback function that will be executed once the common code to detect the device type, network connection, etc., has finished working. This will enable you to use the same process in many future recipes.

Discussion

Because the application is using jQuery mobile, you must reorganize some of the existing code in order to improve code loading. When you navigate between pages using jQuery mobile, it performs the request via AJAX and strips all of the content from the HTML file (unless it is within a `div` tag that contains a `data-role` of type *page*). This means that the previous `window.onload` event will no longer trigger. Instead, a new event that is provided by the jQuery mobile library will be used.

The first thing to note is that the *index.html* page from "Creating a Persistent Navigation System" on page 5 requires some reformatting as follows:

```html
<!DOCTYPE HTML>
<html>
<head>
    <title>PhoneGap</title>
    <link rel="stylesheet"
        href="css/jquery.mobile-1.0rc1.min.css" />
    <script type="text/javascript" charset="utf-8"
        src="scripts/phonegap-1.0.0.js"></script>
</head>
<body>
    <div data-role="page" id="index-page">
        <h1>Hello World!</h1>

        <div data-role="footer" data-position="fixed">
            <div data-role="navbar">
                <ul>
                    <li><a href="index.html"
class="ui-btn-active">Home</a></li>
                        <li><a href="about.html">About</a></li>
                    </ul>
            </div>
        </div>
    </div>

    <script type="text/javascript" charset="utf-8"
        src="scripts/jquery-1.6.4.min.js"></script>
    <script type="text/javascript" charset="utf-8"
        src="scripts/jquery.mobile-1.0rc1.min.js"></script>
    <script type="text/javascript" charset="utf-8"
        src="scripts/common.js"></script>
</body>
</html>
```

Several things have changed in this code. Most of the JavaScript files have been moved out of the `head` tag. I've left the main PhoneGap file there to ensure that it loads completely before the page does, because anything placed inside the `head` tag must fully finish loading before you continue. Next, a new `div` tag was added with a `data-role` of type `page`. Finally, the previous JavaScript files have been moved to the bottom and the order has been altered. These have also been placed outside of the page `div` tag, because they do not need to be loaded again if the user navigates back to the index page. The order of the files was altered because, in the next example, the *common.js* file will be updated to use elements of jQuery and the mobile library, which must load first.

Within the next example is an updated *common.js* file. It contains all of the code from the first several recipes that performs the following operations: device ready, device detection, and network detection, as well as the new callback feature. The key objective of this expanded code is to allow you to run custom code tied to the name of a particular page, when that page loads.

```javascript
// Global variable that will tell us whether PhoneGap is ready
var isPhoneGapReady = false;

// Default all phone types to false
var isAndroid = false;
var isBlackberry = false;
var isIphone = false;
var isWindows = false;

// Store the device's uuid
var deviceUUID;

// Store the current network status
var isConnected = false;
var isHighSpeed;
var internetInterval;

var currentUrl;

function init(url) {
    if (typeof url != 'string') {
        currentUrl = location.href;
    } else {
        currentUrl = url;
    }

    if (isPhoneGapReady) {
        onDeviceReady();
    } else {
        // Add an event listener for deviceready
        document.addEventListener("deviceready",
            onDeviceReady, false);
    }
}

function onDeviceReady() {
    // set to true
    isPhoneGapReady = true;

    deviceUUID = device.uuid;

    // detect the device's platform
    deviceDetection();

    // detect for network access
    networkDetection();

    // execute any events at start up
```

```
        executeEvents();

        // execute a callback function
        executeCallback();
    }

    function executeEvents() {
        if (isPhoneGapReady) {
            // attach events for online and offline detection
            document.addEventListener("online", onOnline, false);
            document.addEventListener("offline", onOffline, false);

            // set a timer to check the network status
            internetInterval = window.setInterval(function() {
                if (navigator.network.connection.type != Connection.NONE) {
                    onOnline();
                } else {
                    onOffline();
                }
            }, 5000);
        }
    }

    function executeCallback() {
        if (isPhoneGapReady) {
            // get the name of the current html page
            var pages = currentUrl.split("/");
            var currentPage = pages[pages.length - 1].
              slice(0, pages[pages.length - 1].indexOf(".html"));

            // capitalize the first letter and execute the function
            currentPage = currentPage.charAt(0).toUpperCase() +
              currentPage.slice(1);

            if (typeof window['on' + currentPage + 'Load'] ==
              'function') {
                window['on' + currentPage + 'Load']();
            }
        }
    }

    function deviceDetection() {
        if (isPhoneGapReady) {
            switch (device.platform) {
                case "Android":
                    isAndroid = true;
                    break;
                case "Blackberry":
                    isBlackberry = true;
                    break;
                case "iPhone":
                    isIphone = true;
                    break;
                case "WinCE":
                    isWindows = true;
```

```
                break;
            }
        }
    }

    function networkDetection() {
        if (isPhoneGapReady) {
            // as long as the connection type is not none,
            // the device should have Internet access
            if (navigator.network.connection.type != Connection.NONE) {
                isConnected = true;
            }

            // determine if this connection is high speed or not
            switch (navigator.network.connection.type) {
                case Connection.UNKNOWN:
                case Connection.CELL_2G:
                    isHighSpeed = false;
                    break;
                default:
                    isHighSpeed = true;
                    break;
            }
        }
    }

    function onOnline() {
        isConnected = true;
    }

    function onOffline() {
        isConnected = false;
    }

    // This gets called by jQuery mobile when the page has loaded
    $(document).bind("pageload", function(event, data) {
        init(data.url);
    });

    // Set an onload handler to call the init function
    window.onload = init;
```

There is quite a bit happening in the preceding code. I will start at the bottom with the
two events that call the init function. The window.onload code remains as-is and will
be called when the application first loads. By binding the pageload event to the document, I ensure that each time a user clicks a new link, this event will fire when that page
has finished loading. It is also passing the current URL to the updated init function.
This will be used for implementing the callback function.

The init function has been updated to accept this new url parameter. However, since
this parameter is not passed in by the window.onload event, the code checks to see
whether it is a string. When a string is not detected (i.e., on first load), the loca
tion.href is used and stored in the currentUrl global variable. Then, if the variable

isPhoneGapReady is already set and *true*, there is no need to add the listener and wait, so it just calls the onDeviceReady function.

The onDeviceReady function has been slightly reorganized and some of the previous work has been moved into new functions for later expansion, including the newly added executeCallback function.

The executeCallback function takes the currentUrl variable and splits it into parts to be able to retrieve just the filename, e.g., the index. This name is then used to check whether there is a function called onIndexLoad. If this function exists, it is executed.

When you add future pages, you can also add new functions that will be executed automatically once the page loads. These will perform any additional processing required by that page. For instance, if you add an onAboutLoad function, the app will execute it when *about.html* has finished loading.

See Also

jQuery Mobile Events (*http://jquerymobile.com/demos/1.0/docs/api/events.html*)

Detecting When the App Is Moved to the Background or Foreground

Problem

Your application needs to perform a specific action when it is moved either to the background or the foreground.

Solution

The PhoneGap API provides two events: pause and resume, that get triggered when the application is placed in the background and foreground, respectively. By adding a DOM listener for these events, the application can respond to them accordingly, e.g., stop retrieving updates from an external source, save the progress of a game, etc.

Discussion

There is one final update that needs to occur to the *assets/www/scripts/common.js* file. The executeEvents function requires updating to listen for the pause and resume events that PhoneGap executes each time the application is moved to the background and foreground, respectively.

```
function executeEvents() {
    if (isPhoneGapReady) {
        // attach events for online and offline detection
```

```
document.addEventListener("online", onOnline, false);
document.addEventListener("offline", onOffline, false);

// attach events for pause and resume detection
document.addEventListener("pause", onPause, false);
document.addEventListener("resume", onResume, false);

// set a timer to check the network status
internetInterval = window.setInterval(function() {
    if (navigator.network.connection.type != Connection.NONE) {
      isOnline();
    } else {
      isOffline();
    }
  }, 5000);
}
}
```

As mentioned previously, custom events will not work on older versions of BlackBerry.

Now onPause and onResume functions can be created. The onPause function is a good place to stop any timer intervals or watches that are in place, as well as set isPhoneGap Ready to false.

```
function onPause() {
    isPhoneGapReady = false;

    // clear the Internet check interval
    window.clearInterval(internetInterval);
}
```

The onResume function can reinstate the listening that was stopped in the onPause function:

```
function onResume() {
    // don't run if phonegap is already ready
    if (isPhoneGapReady == false) {
        init(currentUrl);
    }
}
```

The onResume function calls the init function, which will reset any intervals and watches as well as execute the callback function on the page to refresh the content.

When I was testing this code, I found the onResume function constantly firing, which is why the init function call is wrapped within an if statement checking for isPhoneGapReady == false.

Using the GPS and Displaying a Position on a Map

Problem

You want to retrieve the device's current GPS location and place a marker indicating the current position on a map.

Solution

One of the most common functionalities in any mobile application is to retrieve the device's location through GPS or WiFi detection and then plot the current position on a map.

To read the device's current GPS location, PhoneGap provides three useful functions: `getCurrentPosition`, `watchPosition`, and `clearWatch`. The second function provides frequent updates to the location as the user moves.

The device's current location is returned via JavaScript objects. This information contains a timestamp of when the coordinates were retrieved and an object that contains all of the pertinent information in the coordinates. This enables the user to plot the location on a map (latitude, longitude, etc.).

The PhoneGap API doesn't provide native support for maps, so the simplest solution to ensure that you support the most platforms is to integrate Google Maps API via their JavaScript API. While this will be a little bit slower, as it requires transferring the maps over the network, it is far less work than extending the application via a plug-in for the various smartphones.

Discussion

To begin, you must create a new HTML file called *map.html* inside of your *assets/ www* directory. This file will contain some basic HTML to display the menu, as well as a placeholder for Google Maps API.

```
<!DOCTYPE HTML>
<html>
<head>
    <title>PhoneGap</title>
    <meta name="viewport" content="initial-scale=1.0,
        user-scalable=no" />
</head>
<body>
    <div data-role="page" id="map-page">
        <div id="map_canvas"
            style="width: 300px; height: 300px"></div>

        <div data-role="footer" data-position="fixed">
            <div data-role="navbar">
```

```
            <ul>
                <li><a href="index.html">Home</a></li>
                <li><a href="map.html"
        class="ui-btn-active">Map</a></li>
            </ul>
        </div>
    </div>

    <script type="text/javascript" charset="utf-8"
        src="scripts/map.js"></script>
    </div>
</body>
</html>
```

The navbar has been updated to replace the temporary *About* example with a new *Map* link, which is set to active in this file. This should be updated in your index.html as well. Near the bottom of this file, a new JavaScript file is included called *map.js*. This file should be created inside of your *assets/www/scripts* directory and it will contain the core of the functionality.

```
function onMapLoad() {
    if (isConnected) {
        // load the google api
        var fileref=document.createElement('script');
        fileref.setAttribute("type","text/javascript");
        fileref.setAttribute("src",
"http://maps.googleapis.com/maps/api/js?sensor=true&callback=" +
"getGeolocation");
        document.getElementsByTagName("head")[0].
            appendChild(fileref);
    } else {
        alert("Must be connected to the Internet");
    }
}

function getGeolocation() {
    // get the user's gps coordinates and display map
    var options = {
        maximumAge: 3000,
        timeout: 5000,
        enableHighAccuracy: true
    };
    navigator.geolocation.getCurrentPosition(loadMap,
        geoError, options);
}

function loadMap(position) {
    var latlng = new google.maps.LatLng(
        position.coords.latitude, position.coords.longitude);

    var myOptions = {
        zoom: 8,
        center: latlng,
        mapTypeId: google.maps.MapTypeId.ROADMAP
    };
```

```
        var mapObj = document.getElementById("map_canvas");
        var map = new google.maps.Map(mapObj, myOptions);

        var marker = new google.maps.Marker({
            position: latlng,
            map: map,
            title:"You"
        });
    }

    function geoError(error) {
        alert('code: '    + error.code    + '\n' +
              'message: ' + error.message + '\n');
    }
```

Quite a lot is happening in the preceding example. When the page has finished loading, thanks to the callback function implemented in the previous recipe, `onMapLoad` is called automatically once the page is loaded. Because the jQuery mobile library is being used, the Google API JavaScript file must be included dynamically; otherwise, it doesn't get loaded properly via the AJAX request.

In case you missed it in "Executing a Callback Function Once the Device Is Ready" on page 13, for subsequent pages loaded via the jQuery Mobile API, a simple `window.onload` will not work because pages are loaded via AJAX. Instead, you need to bind an event for *pageload* that is called by the library once the page has finished loading: `$(docu ment).bind("pageload", onMapLoad);`

Once the Google API is loaded, the `getGeolocation` callback function is executed. This function uses the PhoneGap API to retrieve the user's current location. The `naviga tor.geolocation.getCurrentPosition` function accepts three parameters: the success function that is called once the location is retrieved, an error function to invoke if the geolocation could not be retrieved, and finally some JSON options.

When the geolocation is successfully received, the code calls the `loadMap` function, which accepts one parameter called `position`. This parameter contains the latitude and longitude, as well as several other properties, which are used to center the map and create a marker. The remainder of the example includes some of the sample code provided by Google to demonstrate the use of their API. When you run this example, a new map will be loaded into the `map_canvas div` tag and will center on your current location. Also, a marker will be created identifying where you are.

This feature might not work correctly in all simulators and an actual device may be needed.

See Also

Google Maps API (*http://code.google.com/apis/maps/documentation/javascript/*)

Using the Compass to Help the User Navigate

Problem

You want to detect the direction in which the device is currently pointing.

Solution

iOS, Android, and some Windows 7 devices support a compass that will tell you the direction the phone is pointing in, with a range of 0 to 360 degrees.

PhoneGap provides several functions that work quite similarly to the GPS location, where you can retrieve the current direction the device is pointing in degrees. You can watch this value, and your application will receive regular updates on its position. By using the `navigator.compass.watchHeading` or `navigator.compass.getCurrentHeading` functions, you will receive a `magneticHeading` variable that contains a value between 0 and 359.99 degrees.

Discussion

To demonstrate the compass functions, I'm going to put together a very simple HTML page that contains two images: a compass and its needle. To start with, you need a new HTML page; let's call it *compass.html*. You will want to add a new menu item on your existing HTML pages to link the new page.

```
<!DOCTYPE HTML>
<html>
<head>
    <title>PhoneGap</title>
</head>
<body>
    <div data-role="page" id="compass-page">
        <div style="background:
          url(images/compass.png) no-repeat">
            <img id="needle" src="images/needle.png" />
        </div>

        <div data-role="footer" data-position="fixed">
            <div data-role="navbar">
                <ul>
                    <li><a href="index.html">Home</a></li>
                    <li><a href="map.html">Map</a></li>
                    <li><a href="compass.html"
class="ui-btn-active">Compass</a></li>
```

```
            </ul>
          </div>
        </div>

        <script type="text/javascript" charset="utf-8"
            src="scripts/jQueryRotateCompressed.2.1.js"></script>
        <script type="text/javascript" charset="utf-8"
            src="scripts/compass.js"></script>
      </div>
    </body>
  </html>
```

The HTML is quite simple. I've created a `div` element that contains the compass as a background image and loads the needle image inside of it. At the bottom, I've included two new JavaScript files. The first is a library that will help me rotate the image in my JavaScript code in the upcoming example. The second is the next file that must be created, *compass.js*.

```
function onCompassLoad() {
    var options = { frequency: 500 };
    navigator.compass.watchHeading(rotateNeedle,
        compassError, options);
}

function rotateNeedle(degree) {
    $("#needle").rotate(degree);
}

function compassError(error) {
    alert('code: '    + error.code    + '\n' +
          'message: ' + error.message + '\n');
}
```

Using the automatic callback, the `onCompassLoad` function, I've created a watch to update the compass every 500 milliseconds via a `navigator.compass.watchHeading` function. Each time an update is received, the `rotateNeedle` function is called. Using the jQuery library I mentioned earlier, I rotate the needle by the angle of the device. The results of **degree** is a number between 0 and 359.99. As the device rotates around, the needle will move as well, indicating the current direction.

 This feature might not work correctly in all simulators and an actual device may be needed.

See Also

jQuery Rotate Plug-In (*http://code.google.com/p/jqueryrotate/*)

Using the Accelerometer to Detect Motion

Problem

You want to detect the motion of the device as it moves.

Solution

Similar to the compass, devices running iOS, Android, and BlackBerry 5.0 and above are able to detect the device's current x, y, and z axis movements.

Three functions exist that work in the same way as the compass and GPS location, which allow you to retrieve the current x, y, and z coordinates through the use of the `accelerometer.getCurrentAcceleration` function. The `accelerometer.watchAccelera` tion function allows you to receive updates on the device's position, while the `accelerometer.clearWatch` function allows you to turn off receiving the updates.

Discussion

To demonstrate the accelerometer, I am going to use the new HTML5 canvas tag and make an image of a ball move around with the movement of the device. To start, a new HTML page must be created inside of the *assets/www* directory: *accelerometer.html*.

```
<!DOCTYPE HTML>
<html>
<head>
    <title>PhoneGap</title>
</head>
<body>
    <div data-role="page" id="accelerometer-page">
        <div data-role="header" data-position="inline">
            <h1>Bouncing Ball</h1>
        </div>

        <canvas id="canvas" width="350" height="350"
style="border: 2px solid #000"></canvas>
        <img id="ball" style="display: none" />

        <div data-role="footer" data-position="fixed">
            <div data-role="navbar">
                <ul>
                    <li><a href="index.html">Home</a></li>
                    <li><a href="map.html">Map</a></li>
                    <li><a href="compass.html">Compass</a></li>
                    <li><a href="list.html">List</a></li>
                    <li><a href="accelerometer.html"
class="ui-btn-active">Accelerometer</a></li>
                </ul>
            </div>
        </div>
```

```
        <script type="text/javascript" charset="utf-8"
            src="scripts/accelerometer.js"></script>
    </div>
</body>
</html>
```

The preceding code does three important things. It creates a new canvas tag with the ID of *canvas*, creates an img tag with the ID of *ball*, and includes a new *accelerometer.js* JavaScript file. This script should now be created inside of your *assets/www/scripts* directory.

```
var canvas;
var context;
var ball;

var prevX = 150;
var prevY = 150;
var offSet = 0.05;

var accelTimer;

function onAccelerometerLoad() {
    canvas = document.getElementById('canvas');
    context = canvas.getContext('2d');

    ball = document.getElementById('ball');
    ball.onload = function() {
        // once the ball image has loaded, start the watch
        var options = { frequency: 100 };
        accelTimer =
            navigator.accelerometer.watchAcceleration(
                moveBall, stopBall, options);
    };
    ball.src = "images/ball.png";
}

function moveBall(acceleration) {
    var x = acceleration.x * 100;
    var y = acceleration.y * 100;

    var newX = x * offSet + (1 - offSet) * prevX;
    var newY = y * offSet + (1 - offSet) * prevY;

    prevX = newX;
    prevY = newY;

    // draw the ball
    drawImage(newX, newY);
}

function stopBall(error) {
    // clear the watch
    navigator.accelerometer.clearWatch(accelTimer);
```

```
        alert("Error detecting acceleration");
    }

    function drawImage(x, y) {
        context.clearRect(0, 0, 350, 350);
        context.drawImage(ball, 0, 0, 100, 81, x, y, 100, 81);
    }
```

The preceding JavaScript creates seven global variables. The first three will be used to perform the animation, as they contain references to the canvas, the canvas' context, and finally the image of the ball. The next four variables will be used inside of the moveBall function to help calculate the movement of the ball. The final variable will contain a reference to the accelerometer watch, which will be cleared if there is an error.

Inside of the onAccelerometerLoad function, the references to the canvas, context, and ball are initialized. The source of the ball image is also set; it's a simple PNG image of a tennis ball that is 100 pixels by 81 pixels. When the image of the ball has successfully finished loading, the navigator.accelerometer.watchAcceleration function places a watch on the accelerometer. The result of this function is stored in a global variable called accelTimer. This variable contains a reference to the interval that is created by PhoneGap. It can be used to clear the interval via the clearWatch function, as we do in the stopBall function. This might be necessary if you wish to pause the accelerometer during the application.

Every 100 milliseconds, the moveBall function will be called. This function receives one parameter: the acceleration of the device. The acceleration is a structure that contains four variables: the x, y, z position of the device, and a timestamp of when it was retrieved.

The moveBall function will use the x and y positions to calculate how much movement has occurred since the last retrieval. It will then perform a calculation and call the drawImage function, which will move the ball on the screen. First, drawImage clears the canvas's screen; then it draws the image of the ball on screen in the new x, y coordinates that were calculated in the moveBall function. If you would like some more detail on the context.drawImage function, you can read this article (*http://www.webistrate.com/html5-experimenting-with-the-canvas-for-a-basic-walk-animation/*) I wrote when experimenting with the tag to create a walking animation using an image sprite.

If there was an error detecting the acceleration, the stopBall function is called. This function clears the timer with the navigator.accelerometer.clearWatch function. An alert dialog box appears as well to inform the user of the error.

This code is an excellent start to creating a labyrinthine game using the device's motion sensors.

 This feature might not work correctly in all simulators and an actual device may be needed.

Displaying Table-View Data

Problem

You have a hierarchical list of items that you wish to display in a table, cascading so that when the user selects the one item, the table navigates to another filtered list of items, until the user receives the specific detail view.

Solution

We'll use the jQuery mobile library to display a standard-looking table listing of data that the user can scroll up or down by swiping their finger. When they select an item in the list, the library will then filter the list; once they click on a second item, the detail page will be displayed. This is accomplished by some basic HTML and invoking a data-role type called *listview*.

Discussion

This example doesn't contain any PhoneGap work; however, if you are building a mobile application with PhoneGap and you have any data that you wish to display in a hierarchy, you will most certainly want to display it using the standard table listing that allows the user to scroll up and down with a finger.

To start, create a new file called *list.html*. A link in the existing HTML pages should be added to this one. The following HTML in the file will implement the list:

```
<!DOCTYPE HTML>
<html>
<head>
    <title>PhoneGap</title>
</head>
<body>
    <div data-role="page" id="list-page">
        <div data-role="header" data-position="inline">
            <h1>Types of animals</h1>
        </div>

        <ul data-role="listview">
            <li>Farm
                <ul>
                    <li><a href="#">Cows</a></li>
                    <li><a href="#">Chickens</a></li>
                    <li><a href="#">Pigs</a></li>
                </ul>
            </li>
            <li>Wild
                <ul>
                    <li><a href="#">Giraffes</a></li>
                    <li><a href="#">Lions</a></li>
```

```
                    <li><a href="#">Tigers</a></li>
                </ul>
            </li>
            <li>Pets
                <ul>
                    <li><a href="#">Cats</a></li>
                    <li><a href="#">Dogs</a></li>
                    <li><a href="#">Gerbals</a></li>
                </ul>
            </li>
        </ul>

        <div data-role="footer" data-position="fixed">
            <div data-role="navbar">
                <ul>
                    <li><a href="index.html">Home</a></li>
                    <li><a href="map.html">Map</a></li>
                    <li><a href="compass.html">Compass</a></li>
                    <li><a href="list.html"
    class="ui-btn-active">List</a></li>
                </ul>
            </div>
        </div>
    </div>
</body>
</html>
```

The key factor that implements the list is `data-role="listview"` on the first ul tag. From there, a nested unordered list is created. On each inner list, a link is added to the element that should go to the detail page. The `data-role="listview"` contains a lot of options for customizing the look and feel. For example, a bubble count can appear beside the element, dividers can be added to separate a group of data (this will be used in a future recipe when retrieving a list of contacts), and much more. There is no limit to the number of nested ul tags, in case two levels deep is not sufficient.

Retrieving Contacts in the Address Book

Problem

You want to retrieve and display the list of contacts that the user has saved on the device.

Solution

The PhoneGap API exposes a function called `contacts.find` that accepts four parameters, including the ability to search for a specific contact. By using this function in conjunction with the jQuery mobile library, you can display a list of contacts in a table view that, once a contact is selected, will display the contact's full information.

Discussion

Several new files must be created to accomplish this. To begin, you must create the main contact listing page. Inside of your *assets/www* directory, create a new file called *contacts.html*. This file will simply hold the skeleton HTML that will be populated via JavaScript.

```
<!DOCTYPE HTML>
<html>
<head>
    <title>PhoneGap</title>
</head>
<body>
    <div data-role="page" id="contacts-page">
        <div data-role="header" data-position="inline">
            <h1>Contacts</h1>
        </div>

        <ul id="contactList" data-role="listview">

        </ul>

        <div data-role="footer" data-position="fixed">
            <div data-role="navbar">
                <ul>
                    <li><a href="index.html">Home</a></li>
                    <li><a href="map.html">Map</a></li>
                    <li><a href="compass.html">Compass</a></li>
                    <li><a href="list.html">List</a></li>
                    <li><a href="contacts.html"
class="ui-btn-active">Contacts</a></li>
                </ul>
            </div>
        </div>

        <script type="text/javascript" charset="utf-8"
src="scripts/contacts.js"></script>
    </div>
</body>
</html>
```

Some key design elements have been added in the preceding HTML. Firstly, a new `data-role="header"` has been added just inside the page role. This will display a header bar with the title of *Contacts*. Then an empty ul tag has been added with the previously used `data-role="listview"` attribute, which will be populated next with the contacts. Be sure to go back to your existing HTML files and add the link to the new contacts page!

Then another HTML page needs to be created that will display the full contact information when clicked on. Inside of your *assets/www* directory, create a new file called *view.html*.

```
<!DOCTYPE HTML>
<html>
<head>
    <title>PhoneGap</title>
</head>
<body>
    <div data-role="page" id="contactview-page">
        <div data-role="header" data-position="inline">
            <h1>View Contact</h1>
        </div>

        <div id="contact">

        </div>

        <div data-role="footer" data-position="fixed">
            <div data-role="navbar">
                <ul>
                    <li><a href="index.html">Home</a></li>
                    <li><a href="map.html">Map</a></li>
                    <li><a href="compass.html">Compass</a></li>
                    <li><a href="list.html">List</a></li>
                    <li><a href="contacts.html"
class="ui-btn-active">Contacts</a></li>
                </ul>
            </div>
        </div>

        <script type="text/javascript" charset="utf-8"
src="scripts/contacts.js"></script>
    </div>
</body>
</html>
```

Another header element has been added here with the title of *View Contact*, and an empty div tag has been added with the ID of *contact*. This will be used to populate the contact information inside of that page.

Now the JavaScript must be created. Begin by creating a new *contacts.js* file inside of your *assets/www/scripts* directory.

```
function onContactsLoad() {
    var fields = ["id", "displayName", "name"];
    navigator.contacts.find(fields, showContacts);
}

function onViewLoad() {
    // get the contact by the displayName from the URL
    var fields = ["id", "displayName", "name",
"emails", "phoneNumbers"];
    var options = new ContactFindOptions();
    options.filter = getParameterByName("id");
    navigator.contacts.find(fields, showContact,
onError, options);
}
```

```
function showContact(contacts) {
    if (contacts.length > 0) {
        var contact = contacts[0];

        $("#contact").append("<h2>" +
contact.name.givenName + " " +
contact.name.familyName + "</h2>");
        if (contact.emails.length > 0) {
            $("#contact").append("<h3>Emails</h3>");
            $("#contact").append("<ul>");
        }
        for (var i = 0; i < contact.emails.length; i++) {
            $("#contact").append("<li>" +
contact.emails[i].value + "</li>");
        }
        if (contact.emails.length > 0) {
            $("#contact").append("</ul>");
        }
        if (contact.phoneNumbers.length > 0) {
            $("#contact").append("<h3>Phone Numbers</h3>");
            $("#contact").append("<ul>");
        }
        for (var i = 0; i < contact.phoneNumbers.length; i++) {
            $("#contact").append("<li>" +
contact.phoneNumbers[i].value + "</li>");
        }
        if (contact.phoneNumbers.length > 0) {
            $("#contact").append("</ul>");
        }

    } else {
        alert("Unable to find contact");
    }
}

function getParameterByName(name) {
    name = name.replace(/[\[]/, "\\\[").replace
(/[\]]/, "\\\]");
    var regexS = "[\\?&]" + name + "=([^&#]*)";
    var regex = new RegExp(regexS);
    var results = regex.exec(currentUrl);
    if(results == null)
        return "";
    else
        return decodeURIComponent(results[1].replace
(/\+/g, " "));
}

function showContacts(contacts) {
    var cSort = function(a, b) {
        aName = a.name.givenName;
        bName = b.name.givenName;
        return aName < bName ? -1 : (aName == bName ? 0 : 1);
    };
```

```
        contacts = contacts.sort(cSort);

        var dividers = "";
        for (var i = 0; i < contacts.length; i++) {
            var firstLetter = contacts[i].name.givenName.
    charAt(0).toUpperCase();
            // check if we need to add a divider
            if (dividers.indexOf(firstLetter) < 0) {
                dividers += firstLetter;
                $("#contactList").append(
    "<li data-role=\"list-divider\">" + firstLetter + "</li>");
            }
            $("#contactList").append(
    "<li><a href=\"view.html?id=" + contacts[i].id +
    "\">" + contacts[i].name.givenName + " " +
    contacts[i].name.familyName + "</a></li>");
        }

        $("#contactList").listview('refresh');
    }

    function onError(contactError) {
        alert("Error = " + contactError.code);
        return false;
    }
```

Quite a bit is happening in this JavaScript file. The first two functions, onContacts
Load and onViewLoad, perform a search for the contacts. The first function retrieves all
contacts in the address book. The second function filters the contacts by the *id* that is
passed in via the URL to retrieve a single contact (e.g., to display the full information
about the contact selected from the list).

The next function, showContact, receives the list of contacts from the successful contact
retrieval of onViewLoad. This function then displays some basic information about the
contact. There are more fields that can be added, but currently it will just display the
name, email addresses, and phone numbers for the contact. The full list of contact fields
can be found at the PhoneGap page about contacts (*http://docs.phonegap.com/en/1.1
.0/phonegap_contacts_contacts.md.html#Contact*).

> Be sure to read the quirks about each field carefully, as the support
> between each device varies greatly in some instances.

The getParameterByName function is a simple helper function that is used to retrieve the
id from the query string.

The final function, showContacts, is called when a successful list of contacts is received
from the first function, onContactsLoad. showContacts receives a list of contacts, iterates
through each one, and appends a new list item to the table view created in the

contacts.html file. As a nice addition, the contacts are sorted alphabetically by the *givenName*. This is done so that dividers can be added to group the items by the first letter of the contact's name.

See Also

"Displaying Table-View Data" on page 28

Creating a New Contact in the Address Book

Problem

You want to allow your application to create and save a new contact or edit an existing contact in the device's address book.

Solution

The PhoneGap API exposes a function called `contacts.create` that accepts a structure with the information about the contact. It creates a new `Contact` object that contains a `save` function to add the contact to the address book. When the `Contact.id` already exists, the information is updated instead of creating a new contact. By creating a new form that allows the user to enter information about the contact, when the user submits the data, it will be saved in the address book.

Discussion

The first thing that you need to do is create a new form. Inside of your *assets/www* directory, create a new file called *form.html*. This contains a basic form that will be used to collect the contact's information.

```
<!DOCTYPE HTML>
<html>
<head>
    <title>PhoneGap</title>
</head>
<body>
    <div data-role="page" id="form-page">
        <div data-role="header" data-position="inline">
            <a href="contacts.html" data-icon="delete">
Cancel</a>
            <h1>Add Contact</h1>
            <a onClick="return saveContact()" href="#"
data-icon="check" data-theme="b">Save</a>
        </div>

        <form action="form.html" method="post">
        <input type="hidden" name="id" value="0" />
```

```
<table>
<tr>
    <td>Display Name</td>
    <td><input type="text" name="displayName"
value="" /></td>
</tr>
<tr>
    <td>First Name</td>
    <td><input type="text" name="firstName"
value="" /></td>
</tr>
<tr>
    <td>Last Name</td>
    <td><input type="text" name="lastName"
value="" /></td>
</tr>
<tr>
    <td>Email (Home)</td>
    <td><input type="text" name="email_home"
value="" /></td>
</tr>
<tr>
    <td>Email (Work)</td>
    <td><input type="text" name="email_work"
value="" /></td>
</tr>
<tr>
    <td>Email (Other)</td>
    <td><input type="text" name="email_other"
value="" /></td>
</tr>
<tr>
    <td>Phone (Home)</td>
    <td><input type="text" name="phone_home"
value="" /></td>
</tr>
<tr>
    <td>Phone (Work)</td>
    <td><input type="text" name="phone_work"
value="" /></td>
</tr>
<tr>
    <td>Phone (Other)</td>
    <td><input type="text" name="phone_other"
value="" /></td>
</tr>
</table>
</form>

<div data-role="footer" data-position="fixed">
    <div data-role="navbar">
        <ul>
            <li><a href="index.html">Home</a></li>
            <li><a href="map.html">Map</a></li>
            <li><a href="compass.html">Compass</a></li>
```

```
                    <li><a href="list.html">List</a></li>
                    <li><a href="contacts.html"
    class="ui-btn-active">Contacts</a></li>
                </ul>
            </div>
        </div>

        <script type="text/javascript" charset="utf-8"
            src="scripts/contacts.js"></script>
    </div>
</body>
</html>
```

A Save and Cancel button have been added to the header bar and the various contact fields that are shown in the view page are included in this form.

Two minor updates need to be made to the *contacts.html* and *view.html* pages. The header bar needs to be updated to include Add and Edit buttons in the respective pages that will link the user to the form. Below is the updated header for the *contacts.html* file.

```
<!DOCTYPE HTML>
<html>
<head>
    <title>PhoneGap</title>
</head>
<body>
    <div data-role="page" id="contacts-page">
        <div data-role="header" data-position="inline">
            <h1>Contacts</h1>
            <a href="form.html" data-icon="save"
    data-theme="b">Add</a>
        </div>

        ...
```

And now, the *view.html* file:

```
<!DOCTYPE HTML>
<html>
<head>
    <title>PhoneGap</title>
</head>
<body>
    <div data-role="page" id="contactview-page">
        <div data-role="header" data-position="inline">
            <h1>View Contact</h1>
            <a href="form.html" data-icon="save"
    data-theme="b">Edit</a>
        </div>

        ...
```

Finally, the *contacts.js* file requires several changes and many new additions to handle the adding and editing of the contact. The complete *contacts.js* file follows, with the code for retrieving the contacts as well.

```
function onContactsLoad() {
    var fields = ["id", "displayName", "name"];
    navigator.contacts.find(fields, showContacts);
}

function onViewLoad() {
    getContactById(getParameterByName("id"), showContact);
}

function onFormLoad() {
    var id = getParameterByName("id");

    // if there is an id, load the contact
    if (id.length > 0) {
        getContactById(id, populateForm);
    }
}

function getContactById(id, callback) {
    // get the contact by the displayName from the URL
    var fields = ["id", "displayName", "name",
"emails", "phoneNumbers"];
    var options = new ContactFindOptions();
    options.filter = id;
    navigator.contacts.find(fields, callback,
onError, options);
}

function showContact(contacts) {
    if (contacts.length > 0) {
        var contact = contacts[0];

        // update the link to include the id
        $("a[href='form.html']").attr("href", function(i, href) {
            return href + "?id=" + contact.id;
        });

        $("#contact").append("<h2>" +
contact.name.givenName + " " +
contact.name.familyName + "</h2>");
        if (contact.emails.length > 0) {
            $("#contact").append("<h3>Emails</h3>");
            $("#contact").append("<ul>");
        }
        for (var i = 0; i < contact.emails.length; i++) {
            $("#contact").append("<li>" +
contact.emails[i].value + "</li>");
        }
        if (contact.emails.length > 0) {
            $("#contact").append("</ul>");
        }
        if (contact.phoneNumbers.length > 0) {
            $("#contact").append("<h3>Phone Numbers</h3>");
            $("#contact").append("<ul>");
        }
```

```javascript
        for (var i = 0; i < contact.phoneNumbers.length; i++) {
            $("#contact").append("<li>" +
contact.phoneNumbers[i].value + "</li>");
        }
        if (contact.phoneNumbers.length > 0) {
            $("#contact").append("</ul>");
        }
    } else {
        alert("Unable to find contact");
    }
}

function getParameterByName(name) {
    name = name.replace(/[\[]/, "\\\[").replace
(/[\]]/, "\\\]");
    var regexS = "[\\?&]" + name + "=([^&#]*)";
    var regex = new RegExp(regexS);
    var results = regex.exec(currentUrl);
    if(results == null)
        return "";
    else
        return decodeURIComponent(results[1].replace
(/\+/g, " "));
}

function showContacts(contacts) {
    var cSort = function(a, b) {
        var aName = a.name.givenName;
        var bName = b.name.givenName;
        return aName < bName ? -1 :
(aName == bName ? 0 : 1);
    };
    contacts = contacts.sort(cSort);

    var dividers = "";
    for (var i = 0; i < contacts.length; i++) {
        var firstLetter = contacts[i].name.givenName.charAt(0).toUpperCase();
        // check if we need to add a divider
        if (dividers.indexOf(firstLetter) < 0) {
            dividers += firstLetter;
            $("#contactList").append("<li data-role=\"list-divider\">" + firstLetter
+ "</li>");
        }
        $("#contactList").append("<li><a href=\"view.html?id=" + contacts[i].id + "\">"
+ contacts[i].name.givenName + " " + contacts[i].name.familyName + "</a></li>");
    }

    $("#contactList").listview('refresh');
}

function populateForm(contacts) {
    if (contacts.length > 0) {
        var contact = contacts[0];
        var form = document.getElementsByTagName('form')[0].elements;
```

```
        form.id.value = contact.id;
        form.displayName.value = contact.displayName;
        form.firstName.value = contact.name.givenName;
        form.lastName.value = contact.name.familyName;
        if (contact.emails.length > 0) {
            form.email_home.value = contact.emails[0].value;
            if (contact.emails.length > 1) {
                form.email_work.value = contact.emails[1].value;
                if (contact.emails.length > 2) {
                    form.email_other.value = contact.emails[2].value;
                }
            }
        }
        if (contact.phoneNumbers.length > 0) {
            form.phone_home.value = contact.phoneNumbers[0].value;
            if (contact.phoneNumbers.length > 1) {
                form.phone_work.value = contact.phoneNumbers[1].value;
                if (contact.phoneNumbers.length > 2) {
                    form.phone_other.value = contact.phoneNumbers[2].value;
                }
            }
        }
    }
}

function saveContact(contacts) {
    var form = document.getElementsByTagName('form')[0].elements;
    var contact;

    if (form.id.value != 0 && typeof contacts == "undefined") {
        getContactById(form.id.value, saveContact);
    } else if (typeof contacts != "undefined") {
        contact = contacts[0];
    } else {
        contact = navigator.contacts.create();
    }

    contact.displayName = form.displayName.value;
    contact.nickname = form.displayName.value;

    var name = new ContactName();
    name.givenName = form.firstName.value;
    name.familyName = form.lastName.value;
    contact.name = name;

    var emails = new Array();
    if (form.email_home.value.length > 0) {
        emails[emails.length] = new ContactField('home', form.email_home.value);
    }
    if (form.email_work.value.length > 0) {
        emails[emails.length] = new ContactField('work', form.email_work.value);
    }
    if (form.email_other.value.length > 0) {
        emails[emails.length] = new ContactField('other', form.email_other.value);
    }
```

```
    contact.emails = emails;

    var phoneNumbers = new Array();
    if (form.phone_home.value.length > 0) {
        phoneNumbers[phoneNumbers.length] = new ContactField('home',
form.phone_home.value);
    }
    if (form.phone_work.value.length > 0) {
        phoneNumbers[phoneNumbers.length] = new ContactField('work',
form.phone_work.value);
    }
    if (form.phone_other.value.length > 0) {
        phoneNumbers[phoneNumbers.length] = new ContactField('other',
form.phone_other.value);
    }
    contact.phoneNumbers = phoneNumbers;

    contact.save(onSuccess,onError);
}

function onSuccess(contact) {
    alert("Save Success");
    $.mobile.changePage("contacts.html");
}

function onError(contactError) {
    alert("Error = " + contactError.code);
}
```

The existing onViewLoad function has been changed to call a new getContactById function, because the same functionality is also used inside of the new onFormLoad function that populates the edit form with contact information when the user selects Edit.

When the contacts have been successfully retrieved, the showContact function is called on the view page. This function has been altered to append the contact's ID to the Edit link URL so the contact can be retrieved on the form page.

Finally, four new functions have been added to populate and save the contact. First, the populateForm function is called after the user clicks Edit and the contact has been retrieved. It simply extracts the data from the Contact object and populates the form values. When the user presses the Save button, the saveContact function is called. This works similar to populating the form, but in reverse. The values are extracted from the form and saved in the contact.

A few important things are happening inside this function. If the user is editing the user, the contact must be retrieved and updated; otherwise, a new contact is created through the navigator.contacts.create() function. The name, emails, and phone numbers are special fields because they are created through other PhoneGap Contact objects. The name must be defined as a new ContactName object and both the email and phone numbers must be defined as new ContactFields inside an array, because multiple types can be added.

There are several more contact fields that you can add. See the PhoneGap documentation (*http://docs.phonegap.com/en/1.1.0/phonegap_contacts_contacts.md.html#Contact*) for more information, because not all devices support all of the fields.

The last two functions handle a successful save and errors that might occur while saving the contact. Upon success, the user is redirected back to the *contacts.html* page using the `$.mobile.changePage` function.

 It's important to note that the `$.mobile.changePage` was used and not a standard JavaScript redirect with `location.href`. If the latter were performed, the jQuery mobile library would be lost because no AJAX request is performed, and there would be a fresh load of the *contacts.html* file without the necessary JavaScript files (which are only included in the *index.html* file).

See Also

Adding Buttons to Header Bars (*http://jquerymobile.com/demos/1.0/docs/toolbars/docs-headers.html*)

Accessing the Camera and Photo Album

Problem

You want to allow your application to take pictures with the camera or select one of the user's existing photos.

Solution

The PhoneGap API exposes a function called `camera.getPicture` that accesses the device's default photo application, allowing the user to view and select photos or take a new photo with the camera.

Discussion

To begin this example, a new HTML file is required to display a selected photo from the library or a new picture from the camera. Create a new file called *photos.html* inside of your *assets/www* directory. Be sure to add a new link to this file in your existing files.

```
<!DOCTYPE HTML>
<html>
<head>
    <title>PhoneGap</title>
</head>
<body>
```

```
<div data-role="page" id="contacts-page">
    <div data-role="header" data-position="inline">
        <h1>Photos</h1>
    </div>

    <img src="" id="photo" />

    <div data-role="footer" data-position="fixed">
        <div data-role="navbar">
            <ul>
                <li><a href="index.html">Home</a></li>
                <li><a href="map.html">Map</a></li>
                <li><a href="compass.html">Compass</a></li>
                <li><a href="list.html">List</a></li>
                <li><a href="contacts.html">Contacts</a></li>
                <li><a href="photos.html"
class="ui-btn-active">Photos</a></li>
            </ul>
        </div>
    </div>

    <script type="text/javascript" charset="utf-8"
        src="scripts/photos.js"></script>
</div>
</body>
</html>
```

Once again, there's nothing too special in the HTML file apart from including a new JavaScript file called *photos.js* and an empty img tag with the ID of *photo*. This will be used display the photo afterwards.

You now need to create the *photos.js* file inside of your *assets/www/scripts* folder.

```
var loaded = false;

function onPhotosLoad() {
    // only load the camera selector on first load
    if (!loaded) {
        navigator.camera.getPicture(onPhotoLoadSuccess, onFail,
          {
            quality: 50,
            encodingType: Camera.EncodingType.PNG,
            destinationType: navigator.camera.DestinationType.FILE_URI
          });

        loaded = true;
    }
}

function onPhotoLoadSuccess(photoUri) {
    document.getElementById('photo').src = photoUri;
}

function onFail(message) {
    alert('Failed because: ' + message);
}
```

Inside the onPhotosLoad callback function, the navigator.camera.getPicture is used to access the camera. It accepts three parameters: the callback to invoke upon success, the callback to invoke upon failure, and options in structured format. In the above example, the destinationType option is defined as navigator.camera.Destination Type.FILE_URI, which will return the photo as a file path. This path is then used inside of onPhotoLoadSuccess to set the source of the previously created image.

If the destinationType option is omitted, the default type used is a base64-encoded image.

If you want to allow the user to access the photo library instead of taking a picture, the preceding example would need to be edited to specify a sourceType option as well:

```
navigator.camera.getPicture(onPhotoLoadSuccess, onFail,
    {
      quality: 50,
      destinationType: navigator.camera.DestinationType.FILE_URI,
      sourceType: Camera.PictureSourceType.PHOTOLIBRARY
    });
```

Saving Data to a Remote Server

Problem

You want to upload a file from the local device to an external server.

Solution

After the user has selected a local media item, the FileTransfer class is used to perform an HTTP POST, containing the byte data, to an external server. The external server must expose a web service that accepts and performs the remote saving. (This is outside the scope of this book; however, many PHP, ASP.NET, etc., scripts can be found on the Internet to help.)

Discussion

This example will extend the previous recipe and save the photo that was taken or selected. To start, the previously created *photos.html* page needs to be updated to include a button to save the file. This can be added in the header as follows:

```
<div data-role="header" data-position="inline">
    <h1>Photos</h1>
    <a onClick="return savePhoto()" href="#"
data-icon="check" data-theme="b">Save</a>
</div>
```

When the user clicks the Save button, a new savePhoto function is called that will use the FileTransfer class to upload the photo to a remote server. This new function, as well as two others to deal with a success or fail response from the server, should be added to the existing *photos.js* file created in "Accessing the Camera and Photo Album" on page 41.

```javascript
var loaded = false;
var currentPhoto = null;

function onPhotosLoad() {
    // only load the camera selector on first load
    if (!loaded) {
        navigator.camera.getPicture(onPhotoLoadSuccess, onFail,
        {
            quality: 50,
            encodingType: Camera.EncodingType.PNG,
            destinationType:
navigator.camera.DestinationType.FILE_URI
        });

        loaded = true;
    }
}

function onPhotoLoadSuccess(photoUri) {
    // store current photo for saving later
    currentPhoto = photoUri;

    document.getElementById('photo').src = photoUri;
}

function onFail(message) {
    alert('Failed because: ' + message);
}

function savePhoto() {
    if (currentPhoto == null) {
        alert("Please select a photo first");
        return;
    }

    var uploadOptions = new FileUploadOptions();
    uploadOptions.fileKey = "file";
    uploadOptions.fileName =
currentPhoto.substr(currentPhoto.lastIndexOf('/') + 1);
    uploadOptions.mimeType="image/png";

    var fileTransfer = new FileTransfer();
    // Be sure to update the URL below to your site
    fileTransfer.upload(currentPhoto,
      "http://www.webistrate.com/phonegap/upload.php",
        uploadSuccess, uploadFail, uploadOptions);
}

function uploadSuccess(result) {
    alert("Successfully transferred " +
result.bytesSent + "bytes");
```

```
    }
    function uploadFail(error) {
        alert("Error uploading file: " + error.code);
    }
```

The example includes a new global variable, `currentPhoto`. This variable is set after the user selects or takes a picture. The variable is then checked at the top of the `save Photo` function to ensure that the user selected a photo before uploading.

Next, several variables are created. The first, `FileUploadOptions`, contains the information about the picture. The second variable, `fileKey`, contains the name of the variable that is used by the server-side script to save the picture. The final two variables, `fileName` and `mimeType`, contain the name of the file and the type of file, respectively.

Finally, a new `FileTransfer` variable is defined specifying the photo to upload, the URL to which an HTTP POST should be performed, the success and fail callback functions, and the previously defined options.

When the upload is successful, the example simply presents a success message along with the number of bytes that were sent to the server.

Capturing Audio and Video

Problem

You want to allow the device to record audio or video through your application.

Solution

The PhoneGap API exposes two different functions, one for each type of media to capture: `capture.captureAudio` and `capture.captureVideo`. You can use these functions along with the `FileTransfer` class to save media and upload it to an external server.

Discussion

The following example allows the user to create and upload an audio or video file. To begin, a new HTML file must be created. Inside of your *assets/www* directory, create a new file called *capture.html*. Be sure to add a link to this new file in your existing pages.

```
<!DOCTYPE HTML>
<html>
<head>
    <title>PhoneGap</title>
</head>
<body>
    <div data-role="page" id="contacts-page">
        <div data-role="header" data-position="inline">
```

```
            <h1>Capture</h1>
        </div>

        <input type="button" value="Capture Audio"
onclick="captureAudio()" />
        <input type="button" value="Capture Video"
onclick="captureVideo()" />

        <div data-role="footer" data-position="fixed">
            <div data-role="navbar">
                <ul>
                    <li><a href="index.html">Home</a></li>
                    <li><a href="map.html">Map</a></li>
                    <li><a href="compass.html">Compass</a></li>
                    <li><a href="list.html">List</a></li>
                    <li><a href="contacts.html">Contacts</a></li>
                    <li><a href="photos.html">Photos</a></li>
                    <li><a href="capture.html"
class="ui-btn-active">Capture</a></li>
                </ul>
            </div>
        </div>

        <script type="text/javascript" charset="utf-8"
            src="scripts/capture.js"></script>
    </div>
</body>
</html>
```

The following example creates two buttons: one that will allow the user to capture audio and the other to capture video. A new JavaScript file, *capture.js*, is also included. This file should now be created inside of your *assets/www/scripts* directory.

This file will provide two core functions: initiate the capture of audio and initiate the capture of video. Because these functions work in the same manner, only one success and one error function need to be created. When a successful media file is recorded, the file is then uploaded to an external website using the `FileTransfer` class in a similar manner to the last recipe.

```
function captureAudio() {
    navigator.device.capture.captureAudio(captureSuccess,
captureError);
}

function captureVideo() {
    navigator.device.capture.captureVideo(captureSuccess,
captureError);
}

function captureSuccess(files) {
    // more than 1 file might be returned
    // so perform a loop and upload all of them
    for (var i = 0; i < files.length; i++) {
        uploadMediaFile(files[i]);
```

```
        }
    }

    function captureError(error) {
        alert("Error during capture = " + error.code);
    }

    function uploadMediaFile(file) {
        var uploadOptions = new FileUploadOptions();
        uploadOptions.fileKey = "file";
        uploadOptions.fileName = currentPhoto.substr(
    file.lastIndexOf('/') + 1);

        var fileTransfer = new FileTransfer();
        fileTransfer.path = file.fullPath;
        fileTransfer.name = file.name;

        fileTransfer.upload(file,
            "http://www.webistrate.com/phonegap/upload.php",
                uploadSuccess, uploadFail, uploadOptions);
    }

    function uploadSuccess(result) {
        alert("Successfully transferred " +
    result.bytesSent + "bytes");
    }

    function uploadFail(error) {
        alert("Error uploading file: " + error.code);
    }
```

Just as in the last example, when the media file uploads successfully, the uploadSuc
cess function is called to inform the user that the upload was completed.

One important thing to note: inside the captureSuccess function, a for loop is performed on the files input parameter. This is an important factor, because one of the
options available for both types of capturing is to allow the user to record more than
one file at a time. This is done by setting a limit option as the third parameter for the
navigator.device.capture.captureVideo and the navigator.device.capture.captureAu
dio functions.

See Also

"Saving Data to a Remote Server" on page 43

Notifying the Device with Alert, Confirm, and Vibrate

Problem

You want to customize the standard alert and confirm dialogs or notify the user by making the device vibrate.

Solution

The standard JavaScript alert and confirm dialogs work quite well and are even displayed in the device's style; however, in your application you might want to customize the buttons that appear or even make the device vibrate (like a game controller).

The PhoneGap API exposes three different functions: `notification.alert`, `notification.confirm`, and `notification.vibrate`, which are used to notify the device.

Discussion

To demonstrate the `alert` and `confirm` functions, I am going to override the default JavaScript functions to accept the additional customization parameters that PhoneGap supports. This will allow you to keep using the standard JavaScript syntax you are familiar with, while providing additional customization as needed.

To begin, create a new HTML file called *notify.html* and save it in the *assets/www* directory. This file is just a placeholder so that the JavaScript can be explored and tested. Be sure to add a link to this new file in your existing pages.

```
<!DOCTYPE HTML>
<html>
<head>
    <title>PhoneGap</title>
</head>
<body>
    <div data-role="page" id="contacts-page">
        <div data-role="header" data-position="inline">
            <h1>Notification Tests</h1>
        </div>

        <div data-role="footer" data-position="fixed">
            <div data-role="navbar">
                <ul>
                    <li><a href="index.html">Home</a></li>
                    <li><a href="map.html">Map</a></li>
                    <li><a href="compass.html">Compass</a></li>
                    <li><a href="list.html">List</a></li>
                    <li><a href="contacts.html">Contacts</a></li>
                    <li><a href="photos.html">Photos</a></li>
                    <li><a href="notify.html"
class="ui-btn-active">Notify</a></li>
                </ul>
```

```
        </div>
      </div>

      <script type="text/javascript" charset="utf-8"
        src="scripts/notify.js"></script>
    </div>
  </body>
</html>
```

This file simply loads the new JavaScript file *notify.js*, which should be created inside your *assets/www/scripts* directory.

```
function onNotifyLoad() {
    alert("test 1");
    alert("test 2", handleClick);
    alert("test 3", handleClick, "My title");
    alert("test 4", handleClick, "My title", "All done");

    confirm("test 1");
    confirm("test 2", handleConfirmClick);
    confirm("test 3", handleConfirmClick, "My title");
    confirm("test 4", handleConfirmClick, "My title",
"Play Again,Quit");

    navigator.notification.vibrate(500);
    navigator.notification.beep(3);
}

function handleClick() {

}

// button contains the name of the button clicked
// Windows Phone 7 ignores button names, always 'OK|Cancel'
function handleConfirmClick(button) {
    if (button == 'Play Again' || button == 'OK') {
        // do play again
    } else if (button == 'Quit' || button == 'Cancel') {
        // do quit code
    }
}

// override the built in JavaScript alert function
function alert(msg, callback, title, button) {
    navigator.notification.alert(msg, callback,
      title, button);
}

function confirm(msg, callback, title, buttons) {
    navigator.notification.confirm(msg, callback,
      title, buttons);
}
```

In the callback function onNotifyLoad, multiple alerts and confirmations are performed to demonstrate how it can specify more and more detail during callback. Both functions support a callback method that is executed when the user clicks one of the buttons from the dialog that can perform further processing. For the confirm callback function, the button text shows up as the variable to confirm which button the user pressed.

If you want to set as default any of the variables passed to the `alert` or `confirm` functions, you can alter them as follows:

```
// override the built in JavaScript alert function
function alert(msg, callback, title, button) {
    if (typeof callback == 'undefined')
        callback = handleClick;
    if (typeof title == 'undefined')
        title = "my title";
    if (typeof button == 'undefined')
        button = "click me";

    navigator.notification.alert(msg, callback,
      title, button);
}
```

This is a great way to define a standard customized alert or confirm dialog box for all of your existing alert and confirm tags, with minimal effort. These functions should then be moved to your `common.js` file so they can be accessed from any page.

You might have also noticed two additional function calls at the bottom of the `onNotifyLoad` functions: `navigator.notification.vibrate(500)` and `navigator.notification.beep(3)`.

The vibrate function will make the device vibrate for the number of milliseconds defined as the first parameter. The beep function will make the device play a sound for the number of times specified as the first parameter.

Storing Data to the Device

Problem

You want your application to save files locally on the phone.

Solution

The PhoneGap API provides a `FileWriter` class that allows you to write and save a file on the device. The `DirectoryEntry` class provides a function to load the file to be written.

Discussion

To begin this example, create a new HTML file called *notes.html* inside of the *assets/www* directory. This file should start to look pretty standard. It contains the basic HTML to get the layout and navbar as well as a form that contains a `textarea` to allow the user to enter some notes that will be saved locally to the device upon pressing the Save button.

```html
<!DOCTYPE HTML>
<html>
<head>
    <title>PhoneGap</title>
</head>
<body>
    <div data-role="page" id="notes-page">
        <div data-role="header" data-position="inline">
            <a href="index.html" data-icon="delete">Cancel</a>
            <h1>Your Thoughts?</h1>
            <a onClick="return saveNotes()" href="#"
data-icon="check" data-theme="b">Save</a>
        </div>

        <form action="notes.html" method="post">
            <textarea name="notes" rows="30" cols="10"></textarea>
        </form>

        <div data-role="footer" data-position="fixed">
            <div data-role="navbar">
                <ul>
                    <li><a href="index.html">Home</a></li>
                    <li><a href="map.html">Map</a></li>
                    <li><a href="compass.html">Compass</a></li>
                    <li><a href="list.html">List</a></li>
                    <li><a href="contacts.html">Contacts</a></li>
                    <li><a href="photos.html">Photos</a></li>
                    <li><a href="notify.html">Notify</a></li>
                    <li><a href="notes.html"
class="ui-btn-active">Notes</a></li>
                </ul>
            </div>
        </div>

        <script type="text/javascript" charset="utf-8"
            src="scripts/notes.js"></script>
    </div>
</body>
</html>
```

At the bottom, this file includes a JavaScript file called *notes.js*. Create this file now in your *assets/www/scripts* directory.

```javascript
var fileWriter;

function onNotesLoad() {
    window.requestFileSystem(LocalFileSystem.PERSISTENT, 0, onFSComplete, fail);
}

function onFSComplete(fileSystem) {
    // Load the notes.txt file, create it if it doesn't exist
    fileSystem.root.getFile("notes.txt", {create: true}, onFileEntryComplete, fail);
}
```

```
function onFileEntryComplete(fileEntry) {
    // set up the fileWriter
    fileEntry.createWriter(onFileWriterComplete, fail);
}

function onFileWriterComplete(fileWriter) {
    // store the fileWriter in a
    // global variable so we have it
    // when the user presses save
    fileWriter = fileWriter;
}

function saveNotes() {
    // make sure the fileWriter is set
    if (fileWriter != null) {
        // create an oncomplete write function
        // that will redirect the user
        fileWriter.onwrite = function(evt) {
            alert("Saved successfully");
            $.mobile.changePage("index.html");
        };

        var form = document.getElementsByTagName('form')[0].elements;
        var notes = form.notes.value;

        // save the notes
        fileWriter.write(notes);
    } else {
        alert("There was an error trying to save the file");
    }

    return false;
}

function fail(error) {
    alert(error.code);
}
```

When the onNotesLoad function is executed by the callback, an asynchronous request is made to open a persistent file system connection. When this action is complete, the onFSComplete function is called. The fileSystem parameter is a DirectoryEntry object that is used to open a file called *notes.txt* in the root directory. If the file does not already exist, it will be created. When the file has loaded successfully, the onFileEntryComplete function is called.

The onFileEntryComplete function receives a fileEntry parameter, which is a FileEntry object. This object is then used to create an object of the fileWriter class. The object is stored in the fileWriter global variable so that the saveNotes function can use and save the contents to it.

When the write action has been completed (after the user presses Save), a success message is displayed and the user is redirected back to the index page. This action occurs inside of the `onwrite` anonymous function that appears within the `saveNotes` function.

See Also

"Reading Data from the Device" on page 53

Reading Data from the Device

Problem

You want your application to read an existing file and display the contents in a form for further editing.

Solution

Using a `FileEntry` object, retrieve a `File` object that can be `readAsDataURL` or `readAs Text`, which will return data as a base64-encoded url or as text, respectively.

Discussion

To read the *notes.txt* file that was created in the last recipe and populate the `textarea` with its contents, a few updates need to occur inside the existing *assets/www/scripts/ notes.js* file:

```
var fileWriter;

function onNotesLoad() {
    window.requestFileSystem(LocalFileSystem.PERSISTENT, 0, onFSComplete, fail);
}

function onFSComplete(fileSystem) {
    // Load the notes.txt file, create it if it doesn't exist
    fileSystem.root.getFile("notes.txt", {create: true}, onFileEntryComplete, fail);
}

function onFileEntryComplete(fileEntry) {
    // read the file to preload content
    fileEntry.file(onFileReadComplete, fail);

    // set up the fileWriter
    fileEntry.createWriter(onFileWriterComplete, fail);
}

function onFileReadComplete(file) {
    var reader = new FileReader();
    reader.onloadend = function(evt) {
```

```
        // load it into the form
        var form = document.getElementsByTagName('form')[0].elements;
        form.notes.value = evt.target.result;
    };
    reader.readAsText(file);
}

function onFileWriterComplete(fileWriter) {
    // store the fileWriter in a
    // global variable so we have it
    // when the user presses save
    fileWriter = fileWriter;
}

function saveNotes() {
    // make sure the fileWriter is set
    if (fileWriter != null) {
        // create an oncomplete write function
        // that will redirect the user
        fileWriter.onwrite = function(evt) {
            alert("Saved successfully");
            $.mobile.changePage("index.html");
        };

        var form = document.getElementsByTagName('form')[0].elements;
        var notes = form.notes.value;

        // save the notes
        fileWriter.write(notes);
    } else {
        alert("There was an error trying to save the file");
    }

    return false;
}

function fail(error) {
    alert(error.code);
}
```

Because of all of the work done in the previous recipe, only two small additions were made here. Firstly, inside of the onFileEntryComplete function, the file is loaded into a File object via this call: fileEntry.file(onFileReadComplete, fail). When the File object is loaded, the onFileReadComplete function is called.

The onFileReadComplete function creates a new FileReader object and reads the file as text. An anonymous function is used when reader.onloadend has finished reading the file. At this point, the contents of the file are set in the textarea form field named notes, allowing the user to modify any existing notes.

See Also

"Storing Data to the Device" on page 50

Extending PhoneGap with Plug-ins

Problem

You want to add additional functionality to your application for a specific device that the PhoneGap library currently doesn't support.

Solution

Create a custom plug-in that is added to your application and invoke it with JavaScript via the `window.plugin` command.

Discussion

In this example, I am going to extend the PhoneGap library by creating and using an Android plug-in with the application. The goal of this plug-in will be to read an RSS feed and parse the XML into an array of `JSONObject` objects that will be outputted in the existing PhoneGap application. As I mentioned in the preface, I am developing on Windows using Eclipse, so the plug-in will be for the Android only, but implementing the plug-in is platform independent because it is done via JavaScript. In other words, if you were to download an iPhone plug-in, it could be implemented in a similar fashion.

To create a plug-in, a new Android Project must be created. In Eclipse, select File → New → Android Project. I am going to name the project XMLParser. For the Build Target, select the latest Android API. The "Application name" will be XMLParserPlugin. I've created the package as com.webistrate.phonegap.plugin.xmlparser (update as needed for your package). And finally, I unchecked Create Activity.

Once the new project is added, you also need to add the PhoneGap library to your project. Just like during the initial setup, you can copy the *phonegap.jar* file to a new libs directory and add it to the Build Configuration.

Now it's time to create some Java code (since that is how you create native Android applications).

A core class is needed that will respond to calls from JavaScript. Add a new class called *XMLParserPlugin.java* to your project. This class will extend PhoneGap's `Plugin` class. The contents of this class are as follows:

```
package com.webistrate.phonegap.plugin.xmlparser;

import org.json.JSONArray;
import org.json.JSONException;

import android.util.Log;

import com.phonegap.api.Plugin;
import com.phonegap.api.PluginResult;
```

```java
import com.phonegap.api.PluginResult.Status;

public class XmlParserPlugin extends Plugin {

    @Override
    public PluginResult execute(String action,
JSONArray data, String callbackId) {
        try {
            String feedUrl = data.getString(0);
            extractXMLContent(feedUrl, callbackId);
        } catch (JSONException e) {
            return new PluginResult(Status.ERROR,
"Error parsing URL");
        }

        PluginResult r = new PluginResult(
PluginResult.Status.NO_RESULT);
        r.setKeepCallback(true);
        return r;
    }

    public void extractXMLContent(String feedUrl,
String callbackId) {
        AndroidSaxFeedParser parser = new
AndroidSaxFeedParser(feedUrl);
        JSONArray messages = parser.parse();

        if (messages.length() > 0) {
            Log.d("parse",
"Sending ok result, with messages");
            PluginResult r = new PluginResult(
Status.OK, messages);
            r.setKeepCallback(true);
            success(r, callbackId);
        } else {
            Log.e("parse",
"No results found, sending error message");
            PluginResult r = new PluginResult(
Status.ERROR, "No results");
            r.setKeepCallback(true);
            error(r, callbackId);
        }
    }
}
```

I won't go into too much detail about the Java code because I want to focus on what's needed to create the plug-in. The preceding example contains several important statements to provide access to the PhoneGap Plug-in API. Because the Plugin class is being extended, the execute function must be overridden. This acts as the landing function when the plug-in is called via JavaScript.

The return type of the execute function is a PluginResult object. Since the XML parsing will be done asynchronously, a success status cannot be passed back yet. Instead, the extractXMLContent is called, which when completed will return a success or error message. To avoid blocking the execution of the JavaScript call, a NO_RESULT status is returned.

Inside the extractXMLContent function, a new SAX parser is created using the feedUrl that was passed in. To create the SAX parser, I leveraged a code example from the IBM developer site (*http://www.ibm.com/developerworks/opensource/library/x-android/*).

In the original example, an array of class Message is returned. Because the PluginResult can only be a String, JSONArray, or JSONObject, I updated the code to return a JSONArray of JSONObject objects. Again, I'll gloss over the Java code to focus on the plug-in itself.

Once the parsing is complete, if the JSONArray contains no elements, an error status is sent back to the JavaScript; otherwise, a success message is sent back along with the result of messages.

This completes the creation of the plug-in. If you plan to release the plug-in, you will need to compile it into a *jar* file. This can be done via the jar tool (*http://download.oracle.com/javase/1.4.2/docs/tooldocs/windows/jar.html*). Otherwise, you can simply copy the package into your existing PhoneGap project *src* folder.

If you choose to jar your plug-in, you will need to add it to your *libs* folder and update the Build Configuration to include it the same way you first included the *phonegap.jar* file.

 If you wish to be able to compile and test this code, please download the full source code from the URL provided in the preface.

Next, the plug-in must be included inside of the *plugins.xml* file located in the *res/xml* directory. The following line should be added inside the closing plugins tag.

```
<plugin name="XMLParserPlugin" value="com.webistrate.
phonegap.plugin.xmlparser.XmlParserPlugin" />
```

Be sure to update the package path as required for your plug-in.

Next, you must create a new JavaScript file. If you plan to offer your plug-in, this JavaScript file should be included along with your jar file for others to use. Inside of the scripts folder, create a new file called *XMLParser.js*.

```
var XMLParser = function() {};

XMLParser.prototype.parse = function(successCallback,
    failureCallback, feedUrl) {
    return PhoneGap.exec(successCallback,
            failureCallback, 'XMLParserPlugin', '',
                [feedUrl]);
};
```

```
    PhoneGap.addConstructor(function() {
        PhoneGap.addPlugin("xmlParser", new XMLParser());
    });
```

This JavaScript code creates a new `XMLParser` class that is added as a plug-in via the `PhoneGap.addPlugin` command. A new function called `parse` tells PhoneGap to execute the `XMLParserPlugin` via the `PhoneGap.exec` call. The URL specified by the caller for the feed, `feedUrl`, is passed in as a parameter.

The plug-in is now ready for use. For a working demonstration, create a new file called *plugin.html* inside of your *assets/www* directory.

```
<!DOCTYPE HTML>
<html>
<head>
    <title>PhoneGap</title>
</head>
<body>
    <div data-role="page" id="plugin-page">
        <div data-role="header" data-position="inline">
            <h1>Webistrate Articles</h1>
        </div>

        <ul id="xmlList" data-role="listview">

        </ul>

        <div data-role="footer" data-position="fixed">
            <div data-role="navbar">
                <ul>
                    <li><a href="index.html">Home</a></li>
                    <li><a href="map.html">Map</a></li>
                    <li><a href="compass.html">Compass</a></li>
                    <li><a href="list.html">List</a></li>
                    <li><a href="contacts.html">Contacts</a></li>
                    <li><a href="photos.html">Photos</a></li>
                    <li><a href="notify.html">Notify</a></li>
                    <li><a href="notes.html">Notes</a></li>
                    <li><a href="plugin.html"
class="ui-btn-active">Plugin</a></li>
                </ul>
            </div>
        </div>

        <script type="text/javascript" charset="utf-8"
            src="scripts/XMLParser.js"></script>
        <script type="text/javascript" charset="utf-8"
            src="scripts/plugin.js"></script>
    </div>
</body>
</html>
```

This HTML initializes an empty *listview* that will be populated with the results of the RSS feed. At the bottom of this file, the previously created *XMLParser.js* file is included as well as a new *plugin.js* file. The final step is to create the new *plugin.js* file inside of the *assets/www/scripts* folder.

```
function onPluginLoad() {
    window.plugins.xmlParser.parse(parseSuccess,
      parseFail, "http://feeds.feedburner.com/Webistrate");
}

function parseSuccess(result) {
    for (var i = 0; i < result.length; i++) {
        $("#xmlList").append("<li><a href=\"" +
result[i].link + "\">" + result[i].title + "</a></li>");
    }

    $("#xmlList").listview('refresh');
}

function parseFail(error) {
    alert('fail = ' + error);
}
```

The plug-in is called via the `window.plugins.xmlParser.parse` function. It accepts three parameters: the callback to invoke upon success, the callback to invoke upon failure, and the URL of the RSS feed to parse. When the parsing is finished, the `parseSuccess` function is called with the results. This function simply loops through the results and appends a new `li` tag containing the title of the article from the RSS feed as well as a link to it.

There are already several great plug-ins created by the PhoneGap community (*https:// github.com/phonegap/phonegap-plugins*). Enjoy them for use in your application as well as for learning purposes.

About the Author

Jamie Munro, the author of *20 Recipes for Programming MVC 3* (*http://shop.oreilly .com/product/0636920021407.do*) (O'Reilly), has been developing websites and web applications for over 15 years. For the past six years, Jamie has been acting as a lead developer by mentoring younger developers to enhance their web development skills. Taking his love of mentoring people, Jamie began his writing career on his personal blog (*http://www.endyourif.com*) back in 2009. As the success of Jamie's blog grew, he turned his writing passion to books about web development. As well as writing books, Jamie is currently in the process of starting a new website (*http://www.webistrate .com*) that is geared towards helping web developers further expand their experience with many online examples using MVC3, CakePHP, CodeIgniter, jQuery, Database Optimization, and Search Engine Optimization.

Get even more for your money.

Join the O'Reilly Community, and register the O'Reilly books you own. It's free, and you'll get:

- $4.99 ebook upgrade offer
- 40% upgrade offer on O'Reilly print books
- Membership discounts on books and events
- Free lifetime updates to ebooks and videos
- Multiple ebook formats, DRM FREE
- Participation in the O'Reilly community
- Newsletters
- Account management
- 100% Satisfaction Guarantee

Signing up is easy:

1. **Go to: oreilly.com/go/register**
2. **Create an O'Reilly login.**
3. **Provide your address.**
4. **Register your books.**

Note: English-language books only

To order books online:
oreilly.com/store

For questions about products or an order:
orders@oreilly.com

To sign up to get topic-specific email announcements and/or news about upcoming books, conferences, special offers, and new technologies:
elists@oreilly.com

For technical questions about book content:
booktech@oreilly.com

To submit new book proposals to our editors:
proposals@oreilly.com

O'Reilly books are available in multiple DRM-free ebook formats. For more information:
oreilly.com/ebooks

O'REILLY®

Spreading the knowledge of innovators   oreilly.com

Have it your way.